CW01082818

Original title:

Cherishing Connections

Author: Swan Charm

ISBN HARDBACK: 978-9916-89-133-9

ISBN PAPERBACK: 978-9916-89-134-6

ISBN EBOOK: 978-9916-89-135-3

The Bond Beyond Words

In silence, we share a glance,
A fleeting moment, a sweet romance.
No words are needed, just a sigh,
Our hearts converse, as time drifts by.

Through laughter's echo, we find our way,
In whispers soft, we choose to stay.
Each gesture speaks, no need to voice,
In this stillness, we rejoice.

Beneath the stars, we walk in tune,
Soft moonlight dances, a gentle boon.
In the night's embrace, we feel so free,
Two souls entwined, just you and me.

Every heartbeat, a language of its own,
In every touch, our truth is shown.
A bond unbroken, steadfast and true,
In the quiet depth, I find you.

And when the world seems far away,
Our silent love will always stay.
Through every storm, our spirits soar,
Together, always, forevermore.

Foundations of Friendship

In laughter we built our sturdy base,
Shared moments and memories we embrace.
Through trials and joys, hand in hand,
Together we flourish, a strong, steadfast band.

With trust as our anchor, we never sway,
In darkness and light, we find our way.
A bond that we nurture, day by day,
Forever our hearts in sync, we stay.

Light in Each Other's Eyes

A glimmer of kindness in every gaze,
Through storms of life, we find sunny days.
Your smile, a beacon, guiding the way,
In silence, we understand what we say.

With warmth in our hearts, we shine so bright,
In moments of doubt, you're my pure light.
Together we dance beneath starry skies,
Finding our dreams in each other's eyes.

Our Gentle Ties

In whispers and secrets, our bond takes flight,
In shadows and sun, we share the night.
Through gentle touches, we feel the call,
In simple moments, we have it all.

With threads of affection, we weave our tale,
In laughter's echo, we will not fail.
Together we rise, lifting each other high,
In the fabric of life, you and I.

Paths Intertwined

In the tapestry of time, our paths align,
Through winding roads, your hand in mine.
In every step, I feel your grace,
Two souls entwined in a sacred space.

With dreams that merge, we chart the course,
In unity, we gather strength and force.
The journey ahead, both bright and wide,
Together we walk, in heart, in stride.

Whispers of Affection

In the quiet night, soft echoes play,
Words of love drift, dance and sway.
Gentle touches, heartfelt sighs,
In tender moments, true love lies.

Stars above, witness our vow,
In silence shared, we breathe somehow.
Embers glow, warmth all around,
In life's embrace, affection is found.

The Fabric of Friendship

Threads of laughter, woven tight,
Softest moments, pure delight.
In shared stories, hearts align,
Through every season, love will shine.

Supportive smiles, in times of need,
With open arms, we plant the seed.
Across the miles, connections stay,
In every heartbeat, friendship's ray.

Unseen Bonds

Invisible ties, a world apart,
Yet always close, within the heart.
Silent promises, whispered true,
In every glance, I see you too.

Through stormy weather, we stand firm,
Strength in silence, a quiet term.
Unseen threads, forever sewn,
In every breath, our bond has grown.

Hand in Hand

Together we walk, side by side,
In every challenge, love is our guide.
Fingers entwined, a comforting hold,
In each other's warmth, stories unfold.

The path may twist, the road may bend,
With hearts united, we will ascend.
In laughter and tears, together we stand,
Facing the world, hand in hand.

Heartstrings Entwined

In the quiet of the night,
Two souls find their light.
With a touch, a whispered sigh,
Their dreams begin to fly.

Tangled thoughts like vines,
Interwoven, love defines.
Through laughter, through the tears,
Together they conquer fears.

Each heartbeat plays a song,
In harmony, they belong.
With every glance, a spark,
Guiding them through the dark.

In moments etched in time,
Love's sweet and silent rhyme.
With hands clasped, they traverse,
The world, a vast universe.

As seasons shift and change,
Their bond will never estrange.
Through storms and sunny rays,
Together, they'll find their ways.

The Symphony of Us

In the hush of the dawn,
Two hearts beat as one.
With every note we play,
A beautiful ballet.

Melodies fill the air,
Whispers of love declare.
With rhythms soft and bold,
Our story unfolds.

Strings of laughter ring true,
A song only for two.
With harmony in our hands,
We dance to love's demands.

The world may fade away,
But in music, we'll stay.
Through crescendos and falls,
Our love always calls.

As time gently flows,
In this symphony, we chose.
Together, forever in tune,
Under the glowing moon.

Kindness in the Smallest Things

A smile on a dreary day,
Can chase the clouds away.
A simple act, a helping hand,
Kindness spreads through the land.

In words soft and sweet,
Life feels more complete.
With every gentle touch,
We can give so much.

A note left on a desk,
Can make someone feel blessed.
In fleeting moments shared,
Love's echo shows we cared.

In whispers of the heart,
Kindness plays a part.
A laugh, a fleeting glance,
Can bring forth joy's dance.

For every little deed,
Sprouts a hopeful seed.
In small things, love grows wide,
Together, we'll abide.

Under the Same Skies

Stars shimmer in the night,
A shared dream takes flight.
No matter where we roam,
Together, we are home.

Clouds drift and shadows play,
Yet love will find a way.
With you, I feel the spark,
As daylight meets the dark.

In laughter and in tears,
We'll face all of our fears.
Hand in hand, side by side,
In each moment, we'll abide.

The summer breeze will sing,
As joy begins to cling.
Under skies vast and clear,
You'll always feel quite near.

With hearts open wide,
We'll take on life's great ride.
Wherever we may stand,
Together, hand in hand.

Clouds of Comfort

Fluffy whispers in the sky,
Wrap me in their gentle sigh.
Drifting soft, like dreams at night,
They cradle hopes, a pure delight.

In shades of gray, or white so bright,
They gather storms, then break the light.
A promise held in fleeting form,
They bring the calm, they mend the storm.

As shadows pass, they paint the air,
A quilt of dreams for hearts that dare.
In every hue, they come to play,
Dancing softly, fading away.

The Heart's Embrace

In quiet spaces, love ignites,
A warm cocoon, the heart invites.
With whispers soft and tender gaze,
We find our peace in gentle ways.

Through silent nights and daytime dreams,
The pulse of two, a rhythm beams.
With every laugh and every tear,
We forge a bond that holds us near.

In every glance, a story spun,
Our hearts entwined, forever one.
With every touch, a spark renewed,
In love's embrace, we find our truth.

Sails of Shared Dreams

On oceans vast, we chase the breeze,
With hopes held high, we sail with ease.
Each wave a step towards the light,
Together bound, we take our flight.

The stars above guide paths anew,
In whispered tales, our spirits flew.
With laughter bright, we chart our course,
In every storm, we find our force.

With sails unfurled and hearts aligned,
We navigate the ties that bind.
In every shift, our dreams expand,
United strong, we take a stand.

Unspoken Soliloquies

In shadows deep, a voice unheard,
A silent song, not shared, nor stirred.
Emotions dance beneath the skin,
In quiet realms, the thoughts within.

With every glance, a world unspun,
The weight of words left overrun.
In whispered sighs, our truths may lay,
In unvoiced tones, we find our way.

The heart might speak where lips stay still,
In secret streams, we find our fill.
With every pulse, a tale unfolds,
In silence deep, our story holds.

A Garden of Togetherness

In the garden where we grow,
Hand in hand, we sow our dreams,
Colors bloom, a vibrant show,
Sunlight dances, laughter beams.

With every leaf, a story told,
Roots entwine beneath the earth,
Tender moments, warm and bold,
In this space, we find our worth.

Time flows gently like a stream,
Butterflies whisper on the breeze,
Together living out our dream,
Moments gathered with such ease.

In the shade of ancient trees,
We seek comfort, peace, and love,
Nature's song, a gentle tease,
Guided by the stars above.

As seasons change and petals fall,
We nurture hope, we hold it tight,
In this garden, we stand tall,
Together, we ignite the night.

Mosaic of Memories

Pieces scattered on the floor,
Each one tells a tale anew,
Fragments of what came before,
Colors bright and shadows blue.

In every smile, a memory glows,
In laughter shared, we find our song,
From every heart, a story flows,
Each moment short but never wrong.

Time weaves threads of joy and pain,
Stitching them into our hearts,
Through the sunshine and the rain,
This mosaic is where love starts.

Remembering the paths we've walked,
The whispers and the dreams we spun,
In every word and laugh we talked,
We crafted dreams, our lives as one.

Together, we embrace the past,
In this art, forever melded,
Mosaic bright, our love will last,
With every piece, our souls are held.

Anchors of the Soul

In storms of life, we find our way,
With steady hands, we hold on tight,
Anchors cast when skies are gray,
Guiding us through darkest night.

Friendship strong, a sturdy rope,
Through waves of doubt, we sail as one,
In whispered dreams, we find our hope,
With every dawn, a new day begun.

Hearts entwined like vines that climb,
Supported by the love we share,
In rhythm, we write our own rhyme,
With every challenge, we prepare.

Together we brave the tempest seas,
With courage found in each embrace,
Anchors of love, we sail with ease,
In unity, we find our place.

As time goes on, we cherish more,
Every moment, a precious goal,
In this journey that we explore,
We are anchors of the soul.

The Warmth Between Us

In quiet moments, silence speaks,
A tapestry of heartfelt sighs,
In the warmth, no need for tweaks,
Connected deep, as sunlit skies.

Hands entwined, a gentle touch,
In your gaze, I see my home,
With every heartbeat, love is such,
Together, we are never alone.

Laughter echoes, fills the air,
With every smile, we melt the cold,
In the bond, we know we share,
Stories of love, forever told.

As shadows fall, the stars appear,
We sit close, with souls laid bare,
In this moment, all is clear,
The warmth between us is so rare.

No matter where the road may lead,
With you, my heart will always stay,
In every heartbeat, every seed,
The warmth between us lights the way.

Threads of Togetherness

In woven strands of life we meet,
Each moment shared, a bond complete.
With laughter light and hearts aglow,
Together strong, through highs and lows.

Through storms that test our fragile way,
We find our strength in words we say.
Each thread a tale, a soft embrace,
In love's rich fabric, we find our place.

With whispers soft, our secrets shared,
In woven warmth, we show we cared.
Together we create our art,
The threads of life, stitched from the heart.

As seasons change, we stand as one,
In every rise, in every run.
United by the dreams we weave,
In each other's arms, we believe.

So hold on tight, let's never part,
These threads of love will guide our heart.
Through time and space, we'll always be,
In every thread, eternity.

Moments in Unison

In quiet spaces, time stands still,
A fleeting glance, a heart to fill.
Each moment shared, a spark ignites,
Together dancing, through days and nights.

With laughter ringing in the air,
The joy we share is rare and fair.
Like blossoms bright that start to bloom,
Our joy expands, dispelling gloom.

The rhythm beats, a steady flow,
In every step, together we go.
Moments strung like pearls on thread,
Forever cherished, never fled.

Through whispered dreams and open skies,
Adventures waiting to arise.
In unison, our hearts align,
Moments cherished, yours and mine.

So let us hold these moments dear,
In every laugh, in every tear.
Together, we'll forever roam,
In every heartbeat, we find home.

Embracing the Bonds

In warm embraces, hearts entwine,
A sacred space, a love divine.
With every hug, we heal and grow,
Embracing bonds, our spirits glow.

Through trials faced and mountains scaled,
Together strong, we shall not fail.
With open arms, we face the day,
In unity, we find our way.

Like gentle storms that pass on by,
We lift each other, touch the sky.
In every laugh, a memory made,
In every tear, a love displayed.

As seasons shift and days unfold,
Our stories shared will be retold.
Each bond we weave a tapestry,
Of moments filled with love's decree.

So let us cherish what we hold,
In every hug, in tales of old.
Together strong, forever free,
In loving arms, our destiny.

The Ties That Hold

In every glance, a story told,
Of ties that bind and hearts so bold.
With every tear and every smile,
We journey forth, through every mile.

The ties that hold, a sacred thread,
Through moments shared, our spirits fed.
In laughter loud and whispers low,
The strength we find continues to grow.

In unity, we face the dawn,
With hands held tight, we'll carry on.
Through trials faced, we will not sway,
Our bonds will guide us, come what may.

Through distant shores and skies above,
The ties that hold are built on love.
With every heartbeat, every sigh,
Together we will reach the sky.

So let us honor what we've found,
In every heartbeat, love resounds.
The ties that hold us, strong and true,
In every moment, me and you.

A Tapestry of Memories

Threads of laughter woven tight,
Echoes of joy in soft moonlight.
Faded photographs, stories unfold,
Whispers of love in memories told.

Time flees swiftly, yet we remain,
Carrying treasures, joy and pain.
Each moment a stitch, vibrant and true,
Painting a canvas of me and you.

In every corner, a tale to share,
Silhouettes dancing, light as air.
The past a garden where dreams take flight,
In twilight's glow, our hearts ignite.

Through channels of time, we often roam,
Finding our way, we feel at home.
In every glance, a spark will start,
Weaving our lives, thread by heart.

Tapestries shimmering, threads intertwined,
A legacy held, in love confined.
In each pattern, a heartbeat survives,
Echoing whispers of our lives.

In the Embrace of Kindred Spirits

Beneath the stars, we find our place,
In sacred circles, we share our grace.
Hearts open wide, no walls to defend,
In the embrace of sweet souls, we mend.

Whispers of wisdom float in the air,
Every shared secret, a bond we declare.
Laughter and tears, a tapestry spun,
In the warmth of each other, we become one.

Fireside stories and dreams inspire,
In kindred spirits, we spark desire.
Journeying together, hand in hand,
Navigating life, a wanderer's band.

Each friend a star, in our night's sky,
Guiding us gently as years pass by.
In every heartbeat, a promise we find,
In the embrace of kindred, hearts aligned.

Love transcends oceans, bridges, and time,
In unity found, life's rhythm a rhyme.
Together we thrive, our spirits soar high,
In the embrace of kindred, we learn to fly.

The Dance of Souls

In twilight's glow, we find our beat,
A rhythm of hearts, where spirits meet.
Like a gentle breeze, we sway and twirl,
In the dance of souls, our passions unfurl.

With every step, a story is told,
Messages whispered, both timid and bold.
Hands intertwined, we spin through the night,
In the dance of souls, everything feels right.

Ethereal music carries us high,
Two hearts become one, under the sky.
Lost in the moment, we drift and glide,
In the dance of souls, our dreams abide.

Through shadows and light, we navigate,
A journey of trust, we celebrate.
In this embrace, the world fades away,
In the dance of souls, we choose to stay.

With laughter and joy, we leap and play,
In the dance of souls, come what may.
Each twirl, a heartbeat, a longing fulfilled,
In this timeless waltz, our spirits are thrilled.

Seasons of Understanding

Spring awakens with colors so bright,
Hope blooms anew under warm sunlight.
In gentle whispers, we start to grow,
In seasons of understanding, love's glow.

Summer stretches with days long and bold,
Warmth in our hearts, our stories unfold.
With laughter that dances on breeze's wing,
In seasons of understanding, we sing.

Autumn arrives, a canvas of gold,
With moments of change, life's stories are told.
Letting go softly, we find our way,
In seasons of understanding, we sway.

Winter's hush wraps us in its embrace,
Quiet reflection, we find our pace.
Through frozen stillness, our hearts remain,
In seasons of understanding, love sustains.

As time flows on, we gather and share,
A circle of souls, a bond rare and fair.
Through every season, with open hearts,
In seasons of understanding, love never departs.

Ties of Timelessness

In shadows cast by ancient trees,
We weave our dreams like whispered pleas.
Through seasons change, our roots appear,
In bonds unbroken, we persevere.

The sunset glows with stories shared,
With every laugh, we show we cared.
Time holds us close with gentle grace,
In every moment, love we trace.

As starlit skies embrace the night,
Our hearts entwined, forever bright.
Each memory a thread we spin,
In timeless ties, we find our kin.

When storms arise and winds do howl,
Together strong, we will not cowl.
For in the dark, your hand is near,
With you, my love, I have no fear.

Through every age, we'll walk this land,
Together always, hand in hand.
In every heartbeat's soft caress,
We are the ties of timelessness.

Loyal Companionship

In quiet moments, side by side,
In joy and sorrow, we abide.
With gentle words and knowing glances,
In every heart, true love advances.

Through every storm that comes our way,
We find our strength, come what may.
In laughter shared and silence shared,
A bond unyielding, hearts declared.

In times of doubt, you are my light,
With you, my soul takes joyful flight.
Through every trial, we'll navigate,
Our loyal love, it will not wait.

With every step, we forge our path,
In every smile, we share the laugh.
In all the chaos, you are calm,
With you, I find my safest balm.

So here's to us, forever true,
In loyal bonds, just me and you.
For in this life, our spirits soar,
Together always, evermore.

The Heart's Companions

In a world of noise, we find our peace,
In every glance, all worries cease.
Two hearts in rhythm, a perfect beat,
Together, love, we are complete.

With whispered secrets under the stars,
No distance measured, no life too far.
In every adventure, hand in hand,
Together we rise, together we stand.

Through tangled paths and winding roads,
Our laughter echoes, love unfolds.
In storms we weather, we find our light,
For you are my joy, my endless night.

In sweet embrace, our journey's told,
In every chapter, love unfolds.
With every heartbeat, our promise shines,
As heart's companions, your hand in mine.

So here's my heart, forever yours,
With every breath, our spirit soars.
In every moment, may we design,
A life of love, forever divine.

A Chronicle of Togetherness

In softest whispers, our tale begins,
Two souls entwined, where love always wins.
Each chapter written, with ink of dreams,
In the quiet moments, life redeems.

From sunrise glow to moonlit nights,
Together we chase the fleeting sights.
In laughter bright and tender sighs,
Our chronicle grows, while time flies.

With every heartbeat, pages turn,
Through lessons learned, our spirits burn.
In memories held and dreams embraced,
In love's soft glow, our lives are traced.

With every storm we've bravely faced,
In strength and courage, our hearts paced.
Through trials faced and joy displayed,
A tale of love, forever stayed.

So pen this story, forever ours,
In every joy and in the scars.
For in this life where time can tether,
We write a chronicle of togetherness.

In the Light of Our Togetherness

In morning's glow, we rise as one,
With laughter shared, our day begun.
Through silent glances, hearts entwined,
In every moment, love defined.

Together, we chase the setting sun,
In whispered dreams, our futures run.
Each step we take, a dance in time,
With every heartbeat, a perfect rhyme.

In twilight's hush, our spirits soar,
With every challenge, we crave for more.
Our shadows merge, a tapestry bright,
In the warmth of love, we find our light.

The Fables of Friendship

In tales retold, our laughter rings,
Adventures shared, the joy it brings.
In whispered secrets, bonds so dear,
Echoes of trust, forever near.

Through trials faced, we stand so strong,
In every heartache, righting wrongs.
A tapestry woven, thread by thread,
In every chapter, love is spread.

With open hearts, we face the night,
Together we shine, a beacon bright.
In stories shared, we find our way,
The fables of us, forever stay.

Navigating Shared Paths

On winding roads, we walk as one,
In every twist, our hopes are spun.
With every step, our laughter trails,
Through fields of dreams, where love prevails.

In moments lost, we find our course,
With open arms, a steady force.
Through storms and sun, we journey long,
Our spirits bound, forever strong.

With hands held tight, we cross each bridge,
In every heartache, we take a pledge.
Navigating life's vast expanse,
In every turn, we find romance.

Reverberations of Companionship

In echoes soft, our laughter plays,
In gentle winds, our spirits sway.
Through valleys deep, and mountains high,
In every glance, we find a sigh.

With every word, a song is sung,
In harmony, our lives are strung.
Through shadows cast, we shine so bright,
In companionable silence, pure delight.

In reverberations, love will grow,
Through every season, ebb and flow.
With hearts attuned, we face the night,
In bonds of trust, we find our light.

Echoes of Affection

In the whispers of the night,
Love takes flight with gentle grace.
Every heartbeat feels so right,
In your eyes, I find my place.

Silent promises we share,
Underneath a starry sky.
Moments linger, dreams laid bare,
In your arms, I learn to fly.

Time may fade and shadows grow,
Yet our bond will always stay.
Through the tides of ebb and flow,
You are my light, come what may.

With each laugh and every tear,
Echoes linger, soft and true.
Close beside you, I have no fear,
My forever starts with you.

As the dawn begins to break,
Sunlight sparkles on the dew.
In this dance, our hearts awake,
Echoing love's timeless hue.

Tapestry of Souls

Threaded dreams in golden light,
Weave a story yet untold.
Every stitch feels pure and right,
As our lives in colors unfold.

In the fabric of our days,
Laughter mingles with the sighs.
Every twist, a bright sunray,
Each pattern speaks of endless ties.

Moments cherished, softly spun,
In this quilt of love, we dwell.
Together bright, we shine like sun,
Both in heaven and in hell.

Time's embrace we will not fear,
As we grow like vines entwined.
In this tapestry so dear,
Our hearts echo to the blind.

With each thread that we create,
Magic lingers in the seams.
Two souls dance, it's never late,
For together, we weave dreams.

Beyond the Horizon of Us

Where the sky meets ocean's edge,
Waves of passion kiss the shore.
In our hearts, a whispered pledge,
To find forever, evermore.

Sunsets paint our hopes in gold,
As we chase the fading light.
In the night, our dreams unfold,
Guided by the stars so bright.

In the stillness, we will roam,
Hand in hand, through time and space.
Every journey feels like home,
In your smile, I find my place.

With each dawn, new paths await,
Yet our love will never stray.
Beyond the horizon's gate,
Is where our hearts will always stay.

Through the storm and gentle breeze,
We'll embrace what life shall bring.
Beyond horizons, love finds ease,
In the song that our hearts sing.

Shadows Dance in Harmony

Underneath the silver moon,
Shadows twirl in silent grace.
In the night, a haunting tune,
Finds its rhythm, finds its place.

Every step, a soft advance,
Echoes of a love so sweet.
In this dreamlike, tender dance,
Hearts entwined, they skip a beat.

Whispers twine in twilight's glow,
Every glance ignites the fire.
In the dark, our passions flow,
Guided by our true desire.

As the stars begin to fade,
Shadows linger, close and tight.
In this warmth we have portrayed,
Love reveals its purest light.

Let us sway through night and dawn,
Holding close what we create.
In the dusk, love's never gone,
Shadows dance, eternally fate.

Moments in Harmony

In the quiet dawn's embrace,
Birds sing melodies so sweet.
Nature breathes in soft rhythms,
Life dances to a gentle beat.

Sunlight spills on waving fields,
Golden hues ignite the day.
Every moment, every glance,
Finds its path in light's replay.

Leaves whisper in the cool breeze,
Secrets of a world so vast.
Time slows down in perfect peace,
A symphony of shadows cast.

Hearts entwined in pure delight,
Knowing smiles share tender grace.
In this space of shared joy,
Life blooms in a warm embrace.

Moments linger, cherished, rare,
Painting memories like art.
Harmony in every breath,
Together, never apart.

Portraits of Togetherness

In every laugh, a story told,
Each shared glance a treasure found.
Together we paint life's canvas,
In colors vibrant and profound.

Hand in hand, we walk through time,
Creating paths only we see.
Every step is filled with trust,
In the bond of you and me.

Wisdom shared in quiet nights,
Silhouettes against the moon.
In our hearts, the echoes stay,
A familiar, soothing tune.

Seasons change, but we remain,
Roots deep where love has grown.
In every portrait of our days,
Together we have always known.

Through the storms and sunny skies,
We find laughter in the tears.
Every memory intertwined,
Bonding us through all the years.

Secrets of Shared Silences

In the stillness of the night,
Words unspoken fill the air.
Whispers dance in quietude,
A language forged beyond compare.

Eyes converse where voices fade,
Stories linger in each look.
Together in the sacred hush,
Every moment is a book.

Comfort found in gentle pauses,
Breathing life without a sound.
Embracing what we cannot say,
In this silence, love is crowned.

Hearts align in tranquil trust,
In the softness, we unwind.
Secrets held in quiet spaces,
Echoes of our souls combined.

Every heartbeat sings our tune,
Together in this sacred space.
Silence weaves a tapestry,
Of connection, warmth, and grace.

Whispers of the Heart

In the depths where feelings dwell,
Whispers rise like morning light.
Secrets shared in gentle tones,
Illuminate the starry night.

Every heartbeat, a soft song,
Carried on the wings of dreams.
In this dance of souls entwined,
Love flows like gentle streams.

Touch is where our stories start,
Fingers trace the lines of fate.
In a glance, a world unfolds,
With the weight of love, we wait.

Through the silence, we discover,
What the heart has always known.
In the whispers soft and sweet,
Forever, we are not alone.

Together, we weave our tales,
With threads of laughter, joy, and tears.
In the whispers of the heart,
We find solace through the years.

Gardens of Gratitude

In the morning light so bright,
Petals dance with pure delight.
Whispers of the dawn arise,
Nature's gifts in every size.

Hands that sow the seeds of care,
Tend to blooms beyond compare.
Roots entwined beneath the ground,
In this haven, peace is found.

Colors blend in harmony,
Each flower sings a melody.
In the stillness, hearts align,
Grateful souls in every sign.

When the day starts to fade,
In the night, memories made.
Starlit skies, a gentle guide,
In this garden, love abides.

So let us walk this path of grace,
Finding joy in every space.
For each moment we hold dear,
Gardens bloom when hearts draw near.

Soulful Encounters

In a crowded room we meet,
Eyes connect; our souls retreat.
Words unspoken linger near,
In this moment, all is clear.

Shared laughter, a gentle sound,
In each heartbeat, magic found.
Stories woven, threads of fate,
In this dance, it's never late.

Paths together, fleeting, fast,
Yet these bonds are meant to last.
Through the highs and through the lows,
Timeless winds of friendship blow.

With each glance, we seem to know,
In the silence, love will grow.
Soul connections, pure and bright,
Guiding us like stars at night.

Every smile a sacred trace,
Every hug a warm embrace.
In the tapestry of time,
Soulful encounters feel divine.

The Language of Bonds

In whispers soft, the truth is shared,
Through gentle gestures, hearts are bared.
Unspoken ties that bind us close,
In this silence, love is prose.

A glance exchanged, a knowing smile,
In each moment, we reconcile.
Stories told without a word,
In this dance, our souls are stirred.

Through trials faced, we find our way,
In unity, we choose to stay.
Threads of trust weave strong and fine,
In this fabric, hearts entwine.

When shadows fall upon our path,
In laughter shared, we find the math.
Together we rise, hand in hand,
In this language, we will stand.

The bonds we forge, a sturdy strand,
Of love and empathy so grand.
In each heartbeat, let it be known,
The language of bonds feels like home.

Mosaic of Moments

In the tapestry of days gone by,
Each moment shines, a fleeting sigh.
Pieces scattered, bright and bold,
In our memories, tales unfold.

Laughs shared under a starlit sky,
Whispers of dreams as time drifts by.
Colors blend in joyful array,
A mosaic formed in life's ballet.

Through the struggles and through the grace,
Each experience leaves a trace.
Moments cherished, tender and true,
Paint the canvas of me and you.

From sunrise splendor to sunset glow,
In every heartbeat, love will flow.
Fragments of joy and tears that spark,
Mosaic moments light the dark.

So let us gather, piece by piece,
In this creation, we find peace.
For in each moment, bright and small,
A mosaic of life connects us all.

Nestled in Affection

In shadows soft, we find our place,
Wrapped in warmth, a sweet embrace.
Whispers shared beneath the stars,
Our hearts align, no distance bars.

Fingers entwined, we walk the line,
In silent moments, love will shine.
Through storms and calm, we hold so tight,
Nestled close, our souls take flight.

The world outside may cause a stir,
But in your eyes, there's no deter.
Cocooned in trust, we softly breathe,
In tender care, our hearts weave.

Time dances on, yet we remain,
In laughter's song and even pain.
Each glance exchanged, a promise made,
In affection's nest, we are unafraid.

Forever safe, through night and day,
In love's embrace, we choose to stay.
A haven built with every sigh,
Together still, just you and I.

The Warmth of Familiarity

In morning light, a smile appears,
The gentle sound of laughter cheers.
Moments wrapped in sweet delight,
In familiar hugs, the world feels right.

A quiet glance, a knowing sigh,
In every glance, a soft reply.
With every word, our spirits sing,
In warmth, we find our everything.

The comfort found in each routine,
In simple joys, the spaces between.
Sharing stories, both new and old,
In familiar arms, the heart feels bold.

Through seasons flowing, hand in hand,
In every heartbeat, love will stand.
No greater gift, no sweeter call,
Than the warmth of you, my all in all.

So here we are, in sweet repose,
With every moment that gently grows.
In this cocoon of love we share,
The warmth of us, beyond compare.

In the Circle of Trust

Within this space, we find our ground,
A circle formed, where love is found.
In eyes that gleam, and hearts that bind,
A sacred pact, in trust, we find.

Whispers float upon the breeze,
In every laugh, the tension frees.
This bond we cherish, firm and true,
In every heartbeat, just me and you.

Through trials faced, we stand so tall,
In unity, we never fall.
With open hearts, we share our dreams,
In the circle's warmth, our spirit beams.

Each story told, a thread so fine,
In woven tales, our lives entwine.
A refuge built from love and care,
In trust we thrive, no need to spare.

Let's build a life, hand in hand,
Create a world that understands.
In this circle, we are complete,
Together strong, with love's heartbeat.

Bonds Beyond the Horizon

Across the sea where the sun meets sky,
Our hearts take wing, as dreams fly high.
In whispered winds, our stories blend,
A bond unbroken that won't bend.

The distance stretches, yet love holds tight,
In every star that fills the night.
With every heartbeat, we remain,
Connected still, through joy and pain.

Adventures wait beyond the shore,
In every journey, we seek for more.
With each new step, we pave the way,
Bonds crafted strong from day to day.

Beyond the horizon, where shadows dance,
We take the leap, we seize the chance.
In every sunset shared, we find,
A bond that echoes, redefined.

So here we stand, two souls aligned,
Creating memories, softly twined.
Together always, ever so bold,
Bonds forged in love, a tale retold.

Moments that Matter

In quiet whispers of the night,
We find our dreams take flight.
A fleeting glance, a gentle touch,
These simple things, they mean so much.

Time etches lines upon our face,
Yet love remains, a warm embrace.
Through laughter shared and tears we weep,
In these small moments, joy runs deep.

The echoes of our stories blend,
In every start, in every end.
A promise made, a vow to hold,
In every heart, a tale unfolds.

The ticking clock may fade away,
But memories glow, they brightly stay.
In golden rays of a sunset hue,
We cherish all the things we do.

So hold these moments, keep them near,
For in our hearts, they persevere.
With every breath, with each new day,
We make the most, come what may.

A Canvas of Togetherness

Two minds merge, colors collide,
On this canvas, we're side by side.
With every brushstroke, love we share,
A masterpiece we build with care.

In laughter's hue, in sorrow's gray,
Each moment paints a different way.
With lines that weave through thick and thin,
Our story's painted from within.

A splash of joy, a dash of pain,
In every storm, there's sun again.
Together through the highs and lows,
In this art, our love still grows.

Each memory framed, a treasure found,
In silence shared, in joyous sound.
With every pigment, bold and bright,
Our canvas blooms with pure delight.

So let us cherish what we create,
In colors deep, we celebrate.
For on this canvas, there's no end,
In every stroke, our hearts extend.

Sunlight on Our Paths

Beneath the sky, where shadows play,
We walk together, come what may.
The sunlight warms our faces bright,
Guiding us gently, day and night.

Through tangled paths and open fields,
The beauty of life softly yields.
With every step, we share the glow,
In every moment, love does grow.

The whispers of the breeze surround,
With every heartbeat, joy is found.
In laughter's light and silken air,
We find our dreams, a world to share.

As seasons change and time drifts by,
We'll hold each other, you and I.
For through the shadows, light will shine,
Together, dear, our hearts align.

So let us tread this earth as one,
With every sunset, and rising sun.
For in the warmth of love's embrace,
We'll find our light, our sacred space.

The Cradle of Memories

In the cradle of our yesterdays,
Lies a tapestry of golden rays.
Threads of laughter, woven tight,
Each moment shines, a guiding light.

The scent of childhood fills the air,
With tales of joy and lessons rare.
In every corner, echoes roam,
Of times we cherished, called us home.

Through pages worn and stories shared,
The heart remembers, always cared.
A picture's worth, a gaze divine,
Reminds us of the love entwined.

As seasons pass and years unfold,
We gather warmth in memories old.
Each glance exchanged, a gentle trace,
In this embrace, we find our place.

So let us hold what time can't steal,
The tender moments, the love we feel.
In the cradle, let our spirits soar,
For memories bloom forevermore.

Interwoven Journeys

Across the winding paths we tread,
With stories spun and dreams so red.
Life's tapestry in colors bright,
Together we weave, chasing the light.

In laughter's echo, a bond we find,
Through valleys deep, our hearts aligned.
Each step a thread, each moment dear,
In shared adventures, we conquer fear.

The rivers flow where whispers guide,
In hidden corners, side by side.
With hands linked strong, we push and strive,
In every heartbeat, our dreams alive.

As seasons change and time rolls on,
We hold the memories, a cherished song.
Through storms that rage and skies so blue,
Interwoven journeys, I walk with you.

A canvas rich with moments shared,
In silence held, in love declared.
Our footprints guide through dusk and dawn,
In this great journey, we are drawn.

The Unseen Threads

In shadows cast, where secrets lie,
Unseen threads connect you and I.
A gentle pull, a silent call,
In whispered winds, we feel it all.

Through serendipity's sweet embrace,
We wander forth, a fleeting chase.
In crowded rooms, we find our space,
Two souls adrift through time and place.

Invisible ties, a bond so rare,
Every glance shared, a moment laid bare.
With hearts entwined in cosmic dance,
We navigate fate's subtle chance.

The magic lies beneath the skin,
In every loss, in every win.
Together we trace the lines of fate,
The unseen threads that love creates.

So here we stand, where life unfolds,
In every story, new and old.
With faith in paths that cross again,
The unseen threads forever remain.

A Quilt of Smiles

In every patch, a story sewn,
A quilt of smiles, love overgrown.
Colors splash like laughter bright,
Warmth surrounds in the fading light.

Each square a moment, stitched with care,
In memory's fabric, we find ourselves there.
Stitched by hands that never tire,
In joyful gatherings, we spark the fire.

Through seasons passed and seasons bold,
We drape the warmth that never grows old.
A tender hug on a winter's eve,
In every seam, we dare to believe.

With every tear, a lesson learned,
In every patch, a flame that burned.
Together we dance through joy and strife,
In this quilt of smiles, we weave our life.

So hold it close, this treasured blend,
In woven stories, my dearest friend.
A quilt of smiles, forever to keep,
In dreamy nights, in whispers deep.

Beneath the Canopy of Us

Beneath the canopy, where shadows play,
We carve our path in the light of day.
Whispers of leaves tell tales so sweet,
In the quiet moments, our hearts meet.

The sunlight filters through branches wide,
In this haven, we turn the tide.
Soft breezes carry our laughter high,
While dreams take flight in the open sky.

In every rustle, a memory calls,
As nature's magic in silence falls.
The roots run deep, anchoring us firm,
In this sanctuary, our spirits warm.

We dance in circles, lost in the bliss,
With every glance, a moment we kiss.
Under the stars, our promises glow,
Beneath the canopy, love's gentle flow.

As twilight fades to a soft embrace,
We trust this place, our sacred space.
Together we stand, through thick and thin,
Beneath the canopy, new journeys begin.

The Language of Laughter

In a room filled with cheer,
Giggles dance in the air.
Whispers of joy weave near,
Laughter breaks every care.

Like music, it flows so free,
A melody shared with friends.
Bringing hearts to agree,
Where every sorrow mends.

Echoing through the night,
Bright stars mirror our glee.
In moments pure and light,
Together we can be.

From whispers to roaring sounds,
We find solace in the play.
Life's humor knows no bounds,
Healing in its own way.

So let the laughter ring,
As smiles paint the scene.
In this joy, we take wing,
Sowing peace, evergreen.

Hand in Hand Through Time

Through every twist and turn,
We walk the paths we make.
With lessons we now learn,
Together hearts awake.

Seasons change, yet we stay,
Side by side, hand in hand.
Guided by love's bright ray,
In a world so grand.

The years may come and go,
With memories we embrace.
In the ebb and the flow,
Time cannot erase.

Every laughter, every tear,
Threads woven in our tale.
Whispered dreams that we steer,
Together we set sail.

So here's to all we share,
Moments soft as a sigh.
In life, beyond compare,
With you, I learn to fly.

Tides of Kindred Spirits

In the soft moon's glow,
Waves kiss the sandy shore.
Together, ebb and flow,
Hearts longing for more.

Whispers in the breeze sing,
Of bonds that time can't fray.
With every tide we bring,
Love carries us away.

Footprints washed from the land,
Yet memories remain bright.
In this life, hand in hand,
We dance in the starlight.

Like seashells, unique we stand,
Treasured finds on the path.
Kindred spirits, our strand,
Guided by love's sweet math.

As oceans shift and sway,
We find our anchor true.
In tides that come to play,
Forever, me and you.

Memories Woven in Sunshine

Under the golden rays,
We gather, hearts aglow.
In laughter's soft embrace,
Time dances, swift and slow.

Summer's warmth on our skin,
Recalling days gone past.
In the light, love's akin,
Moments built to last.

Each shadow tells a tale,
Of dreams as bright as day.
With every spoken scale,
The heart finds its way.

Embers of joy ignite,
Through seasons that we roam.
Memories live so bright,
In the heart, we find home.

So let the sun pour down,
Wrapping us in its glow.
With memories we've sown,
In sunshine, love will grow.

Threads of Togetherness

In a tapestry woven tight,
Strands of hope glimmer bright.
We stitch our dreams, one by one,
Together we rise, we have just begun.

The laughter shared, a joyful sound,
In every corner, love is found.
Through trials faced, hand in hand,
In unity's strength, together we stand.

Woven hearts in life's embrace,
Every moment, a sacred space.
Threads of trust, soft and warm,
In each other's arms, we find our form.

A quilt of memories, rich and vast,
Stories of present and shadows of past.
In every stitch, a tale to tell,
Bound by love, we know it well.

Together we dance, the world our stage,
Turning the page, life's sweet wage.
In this journey, our paths entwined,
Threads of togetherness, ever aligned.

Beneath the Same Stars

Under the blanket of the night,
Whispers of dreams take flight.
Each star twinkles, a silver spark,
Binding our fates in the dark.

Thoughts like fireflies, soft and bright,
Carry our hopes through the night.
Connected by wishes cast afar,
Guided by love, beneath the same star.

Through the silence, our hearts converse,
A melody sweet, a cosmic verse.
When eyes meet across the sea,
We find our place, where we are free.

In moments shared, our spirits shine,
Time stands still, feeling divine.
Each heartbeat echoes, a silent choir,
Igniting our souls with endless desire.

Beneath the heavens, we dream as one,
Until the dawn brings the rising sun.
In the vastness, we find our way,
Beneath the same stars, love's endless play.

Echoes of the Heart

In quiet whispers, feelings rise,
Echoes of love beneath the skies.
A heartbeat soft, a gentle sound,
In solitude, our souls are found.

Memories linger in the air,
Chasing shadows, unaware.
With every pulse, a name we call,
Resounding through the night, a fall.

In the silence, secrets bloom,
Filling the corners of every room.
Each sigh a story, each tear a part,
Binding us tightly, echoes of the heart.

Through the journeys, we leave our trace,
Time may change, but love won't erase.
In every echo, a promise stays,
A light that guides us through the haze.

Together we'll weave our timeless song,
Through echoes that carry us along.
In this symphony of life we impart,
The beautiful echoes of the heart.

Ties That Bind

In the fabric of time, we weave our ties,
Threads of kindness under the skies.
With every bond, a story spun,
Ties that bind, never undone.

Through laughter shared and tears we shed,
In moments of silence, words left unsaid.
With every heartbeat, love's gentle call,
Ties that bind us, strong through it all.

A circle unbroken, steadfast and sure,
In the face of the storm, we endure.
Through distances far and trials unkind,
In each other's hearts, compassion we'll find.

With dreams intertwined like branches of trees,
Rooted in love, swaying with ease.
Through seasons of life, as we climb,
Ties that bind in rhythm and rhyme.

Together we rise, and together we fall,
In this dance of life, we embrace it all.
For in love's gentle hold, we find,
The beautiful ties that forever bind.

A Journey of Gentle Steps

Through paths we wander, soft and slow,
Each footfall whispers, where dreams can flow.
The sun dips low, casting golden light,
In gentle moments, our hearts take flight.

With every breath, a story unfolds,
In quiet corners, our history holds.
The rustling leaves, a serenade sweet,
As together we walk, our worries retreat.

Steps in rhythm, a dance of the soul,
With every turn, we find ourselves whole.
The night embraces, with stars on high,
Each glance exchanged, a soft lullaby.

In the stillness, we nurture our dreams,
Lost in the whispers of flowing streams.
Under the moon, with hearts intertwined,
In the journey of life, true peace we find.

So here we stand, on this tender ground,
With footprints of love, forever abound.
In gentle steps, we build our way,
Through the fleeting night into the day.

Radiance of Familiar Faces

In crowded rooms, your laughter shines,
A beacon bright, where comfort aligns.
With every smile, a story reborn,
In the tapestry woven, hearts are adorned.

Echoes of joy in the bonds we share,
In the warmth of your gaze, I know you care.
Each moment captured, memories trace,
An eternal embrace in familiar space.

Through life's seasons, our ties remain strong,
In every challenge, together we belong.
The beauty of friendship, a gift we hold,
In the radiance shared, our souls unfold.

In laughter's embrace or in moments of tears,
Familiar faces will calm all our fears.
With open hearts, we navigate time,
In the rhythm of love, our spirits rhyme.

So here's to the circles that always blend,
To the radiance of faces, our truest friends.
In every glance, a promise we see,
In the dance of our lives, together we'll be.

The Call of Shared Moments

In the whispering breeze, our laughter unfolds,
With echoes of stories that life gently holds.
Each shared moment, a thread in the seam,
We weave through the hours, as if in a dream.

On sunlit trails, we wander anew,
Every glance tells, how much we hold true.
In the stillness of dusk, hand in hand tight,
The call of our hearts ignites the night.

With every heartbeat, a rhythm we find,
In the tapestry woven, our souls intertwined.
Through the joy and the tears, together we stand,
In the dance of our moments, life's sweetest band.

The clock may tick on, but time can't erase,
The magic we carry in every embrace.
In the depth of our laughter, the warmth of our sighs,
We cherish these moments, as time swiftly flies.

So heed the call of the moments we share,
In the dance of existence, with hearts laid bare.
In each fleeting second, a treasure is found,
In the rhythm of life, our love will resound.

Bonds Beyond Measure

In the garden of life, our roots intertwine,
With threads of affection that endlessly shine.
Through laughter and trials, we weather the storm,
In the bond of our hearts, we find our true form.

Like stars in the night, we light up the dark,
With whispers of love, we ignite the spark.
Each moment together, a treasure so rare,
In the fabric of friendship, we nurture our care.

Through pathways of time, we journey and grow,
In the dance of existence, our spirits bestow.
With generous hearts, we embrace the exchange,
In bonds that connect us, we joyfully range.

So here's to the ties that forever renew,
In the warmth of our love, we find solace true.
Beyond measure, these bonds tightly seal,
In the story of life, it's love we reveal.

In the echoes of laughter, in tears that we share,
Bonds beyond measure, a treasure so rare.
Together we flourish, forever we'll be,
In the tapestry woven, just you and me.

Hearts Alight in Silhouettes

In twilight glow, our shadows dance,
With whispered dreams, we take a chance.
The world is hushed, our hearts ignite,
As silhouettes embrace the night.

Two souls entwined, a delicate thread,
Through every laugh, through words unsaid.
In fleeting moments, magic blooms,
Hearts alight, dispelling glooms.

Against the sky, we trace our past,
In quiet vows, our shadows cast.
Though time may fade, our spirits soar,
In every heartbeat, we want more.

The echoes linger, a soft refrain,
In silent promises, we find no pain.
Together we stand, through thick and thin,
In silhouettes where love begins.

So let us wander, hand in hand,
Through dusky paths, across the land.
In every heartbeat, we'll write our fate,
In hearts alight, we celebrate.

The Fire of Familiarity

In the warmth of smiles, we gather near,
The fire of familiarity, our hearts sincere.
In laughter shared, we find our light,
Illuminating shadows of the night.

With every glance, our stories blend,
In the dance of us, we always mend.
Through gentle words, our spirits flow,
In the fire's glow, our feelings grow.

The sparks arise, igniting dreams,
In cherished moments, nothing's as it seems.
Together we've traveled, through thick and lean,
With love like embers, eternally keen.

In every silence, in every sigh,
The fire of familiarity will never die.
With every heartbeat, we choose to stay,
In this radiant warmth, come what may.

So gather 'round, let the stories unfold,
In the fire's embrace, our hearts turn bold.
For in this flame, we find our way,
In the fire of us, forever we'll play.

Leaves of Our Shared Story

In the autumn breeze, our tale begins,
With fallen leaves, our laughter spins.
Each rustling whisper, a memory shared,
In nature's canvas, our hearts laid bare.

The colors burst, like love's sweet glow,
In every turn, through highs and lows.
Together we weave a tapestry bright,
With leaves of our story, an endless flight.

When winter comes, and the skies turn gray,
We'll hold each other, come what may.
Through every season, our roots grow deep,
In the quiet moments, the love we keep.

As blossoms bloom in the springtime's grace,
We'll dance in sunshine, joy on our face.
In every heartbeat, our story thrives,
With leaves of our past, our love survives.

So let the winds carry us along,
In the rhythm of life, we find our song.
With leaves of our shared story, we stand tall,
In this beautiful journey, we have it all.

Voices of Unity

In harmony, we rise and sing,
Voices unite, a joyful ring.
With every note, we break the chain,
In melodies pure, we feel no pain.

Through trials faced, side by side,
Our hearts together, will not divide.
With every whisper, a bridge we build,
In voices of unity, hope is fulfilled.

As colors blend in the evening sky,
Bound by love, we learn to fly.
Through each heartbeat, a promise stays,
Beyond the night, into the days.

In collective strength, we shape our fate,
With open arms, we celebrate.
In every story, a lesson learned,
Voices of unity, forever burned.

So let us gather, in joy and peace,
In the dance of life, our love won't cease.
With every heartbeat, we find our way,
In voices united, come what may.

In the Company of Stars

A blanket of night, shimmering bright,
Whispers of dreams in the soft twilight.
Each pinprick glows, a distant sigh,
In the company of stars, we drift and fly.

Silver trails weave through the vast unknown,
Stories of lovers, paths overgrown.
Galaxies twirl, in cosmic embrace,
A dance through the void, we find our place.

Time melts away in space's sweet hold,
Memories shimmer like stardust, untold.
With every heartbeat, the universe sings,
In moments like these, our hearts take wings.

We reach out our hands to grasp what's true,
Connections made beneath skies so blue.
In this silent chaos, we hear the calls,
In the company of stars, love never falls.

So let us linger, beneath celestial glow,
Finding our peace as the night winds blow.
Together we'll wander, hand in hand,
In the company of stars, forever we stand.

Silent Promises

In the quiet dusk where shadows lay,
Whispers of hope begin to sway.
Promises linger, unspoken yet clear,
In the silent moments, we draw near.

A glance exchanged, a subtle spark,
In the embrace of twilight, we embark.
Every heartbeat echoes a vow,
In silent promises, we find our now.

The world fades away, just you and I,
Wrapped in a warmth as the stars reply.
Faith in the softness, a gentle grace,
In silent promises, we find our place.

Each touch holds a promise, a story untold,
Like gold in the dark, our dreams unfold.
With breath held tight, we dance through the haze,
In the symphony of silence, our hearts raise.

So let the world spin, let the moments fly,
With every heartbeat, our spirits will try.
In the stillness, our truth will arise,
In silent promises, love never lies.

Connections Beyond Words

In a crowded room, we find our space,
Eyes meet gently, a softer pace.
No need for voices, our souls entwine,
Connections beyond words, your heart in mine.

Each smile a whisper, a spark of light,
In the silence, we feel so right.
Beyond the chatter, a truth we share,
Lost in the magic of the midair.

Moments that linger, where time stands still,
In the language of soul, we savor the thrill.
Every heartbeat echoes, a timeless song,
In connections beyond words, we both belong.

The world can fade, but we remain close,
In uncharted realms, love is our chose.
Hand in hand, we wander this bliss,
In the quiet embrace, sealed with a kiss.

So let the silence be our guiding star,
In the depths of connection, we've come so far.
With each fleeting moment, we learn and grow,
In connections beyond words, love's gentle flow.

The Gift of Presence

Beneath the surface, where feelings lie,
In the stillness, we find the why.
A moment shared, the heart's true essence,
In the gift of presence, love's sheer presence.

With every glance, the world fades away,
In quiet corners, where shadows play.
In laughter and tears, we weave our thread,
The gift of presence, where words are shed.

Softly we gather, like leaves in the breeze,
In the warmth of each other, our hearts find ease.
With open arms, we embrace the day,
The gift of presence in every sway.

Time does not bind what love connects,
In moments unmeasured, no need for precepts.
With every heartbeat, we cherish the now,
The gift of presence, an eternal vow.

So let us linger in this sweet embrace,
Finding the light in each other's space.
For every encounter, a treasure we'll keep,
The gift of presence, a promise to reap.

The Bridge of Our Hearts

In twilight's glow, our spirits meet,
Two souls entwined, where echoes greet.
A span of love, so strong and true,
Each pulse a promise, just me and you.

Through storms we walk, hand in hand,
With whispered hopes, we take our stand.
In every heartbeat, a steadfast song,
The bridge we build, where we belong.

In laughter's dance, the shadows fade,
With every tear, our bond is made.
Together we rise, together we fall,
With hearts as one, we can conquer all.

From dawn till dusk, we share the light,
Guided by stars in the velvet night.
Our love a beacon, a guiding spark,
On this bridge of hearts, we leave our mark.

For every moment, both meek and bold,
Within our arms, the world unfolds.
Through the passage of time, we'll forever stay,
On the bridge of our hearts, come what may.

When Souls Resonate

In the silence, a whisper shared,
Two souls align, with hearts laid bare.
A gentle touch, a knowing glance,
In unity found, we take our chance.

Like music played on strings of gold,
The stories of old begin to unfold.
Every heartbeat, a rhythm divine,
In the dance of existence, intertwine.

With every breath, the world stands still,
In sacred moments, we know the thrill.
Connected deeply, boundless and free,
When souls resonate, just you and me.

Under the stars, where dreams take flight,
Our spirits soar, from day into night.
In the tapestry of time, we sew,
The threads of our lives start to glow.

In this symphony, we find our way,
With every note, we choose to stay.
Through storms and sunshine, we'll navigate,
In resonance, our love creates.

The Comfort of Quiet Moments

In stillness found, the world retreats,
A treasured pause as time repeats.
With bated breath, our spirits rest,
In quiet moments, we feel the best.

The rustle of leaves, a gentle breeze,
In nature's arms, we find our ease.
With whispered thoughts and knowing smiles,
In comfort's cradle, we span the miles.

As twilight falls, the stars ignite,
In shared silence, our hearts take flight.
Each heartbeat echoes, a soothing balm,
In embrace, we find our calm.

Through fleeting hours, we weave our dreams,
In the silence, more than it seems.
Each treasured glance, a promise made,
In quiet moments, love won't fade.

So let us linger, just you and me,
In peaceful whispers, forever free.
With time as our guard, we'll softly sway,
In the comfort of quiet moments, we'll stay.

Skies that Envelop Us

Beneath the vast, embracing skies,
Our whispers dance, like clouds that rise.
In shades of blue, our hopes take form,
In every breath, a love so warm.

The sun will set, the stars will shine,
In this vast expanse, your hand in mine.
With every sunset painting the night,
Our dreams take flight, in sheer delight.

Through misty dawns, and twilight hues,
Each passing moment is ours to choose.
In skies that hold our wishes dear,
With every heartbeat, I hold you near.

As seasons change, the sky remains,
In laughter and joy, through loss and pains.
Together we wander, forever plus,
In the skies that envelop us.

So let's explore, just you and I,
With every cloud, we'll touch the sky.
In the embrace of the limitless blue,
In love's horizon, it's me and you.

The Echo of You and Me

In the quiet of the night,
Whispers float on the breeze,
Memories dance in the light,
A symphony of ease.

Through shadows softly cast,
Our laughter weaves a thread,
In moments that can't last,
But linger in the head.

Time weaves its gentle spell,
Yet love remains in sight,
In every story we tell,
Our hearts take their flight.

Bound by unseen ties,
Two souls in harmony,
In the truth of our eyes,
The echo of you and me.

As dawn breaks the night's hold,
We rise with the sun's grace,
New adventures unfold,
Yet we find our place.

Fortress of Familiarity

In the walls of this abode,
Laughter and love entwine,
Stories in every code,
Our hearts forever shine.

Windows to our shared dreams,
Each room holds a tale,
Through sunlight's gentle beams,
Together we prevail.

Within these sacred halls,
Comfort and peace reside,
Where the heart never falls,
And love becomes our guide.

Through the storms we stand tall,
United, never weak,
In this fortress, we call,
Home, where spirits speak.

As seasons shift and sway,
Our bond grows ever strong,
In this sacred ballet,
Together we belong.

Kinship's Gentle Touch

In the fabric of our days,
Threads of laughter intertwine,
Woven in so many ways,
In love, we truly shine.

With each shared glance or smile,
A language we both know,
In moments that beguile,
Together, we both grow.

Through trials, side by side,
With hands clasped, we endure,
With kinship as our guide,
Our hearts stay warm and pure.

In whispers soft and light,
We find our silent strength,
In every starry night,
The depth of love's great length.

As seasons come and go,
We cherish each embrace,
In kinship's gentle glow,
Our hearts find their true place.

A Chorus of Togetherness

In harmony, we sing,
Voices blend, pure and bright,
In this joyful offering,
We find our shared delight.

Each note, a piece of heart,
Resonating with the soul,
In this world, we take part,
Together, we are whole.

Through crescendos we rise,
United, hand in hand,
Our spirits reach the skies,
In this boundless land.

With each gentle refrain,
We weave a melody,
In love, we find the gain,
A sweet, eternal spree.

As the last chord does fade,
We cherish every sound,
In this chorus we've made,
Together, love's profound.

Our Unbreakable Link

In the silence, we find our way,
Connected souls, come what may.
A bond that time cannot sever,
In every storm, we are forever.

Through trials that life tends to bring,
We stand united, facing everything.
A thread of warmth that never fades,
Together we dance in light and shades.

In laughter, we rise, in tears, we heal,
Our hearts, like armor, strong and real.
In whispered dreams, our hopes entwined,
An unbreakable link, beautifully designed.

Starlit Connections

Under the stars, our spirits soar,
Each twinkle a promise, forevermore.
A universe crafted in midnight hues,
With each heartbeat, I choose you.

Galaxies spin with every glance,
In this cosmic dance, we take our chance.
Fleeting moments, yet timeless we are,
Closer than constellations, near and far.

In the dark, your glow is bright,
Guiding my path, a beacon of light.
Together we share this celestial stream,
Starlit connections, as vivid as dreams.

The Space We Share

In the quiet, a spark ignites,
A realm of wonders, endless sights.
Between us lies a gentle space,
Where time stands still, a sacred place.

With every word, we plant a seed,
In this garden of love, we both feed.
A tapestry woven with care and grace,
The warmth of your smile, my favorite place.

In moments stolen, our laughter rings,
The melody of life and all it brings.
Together we navigate this vast affair,
In the heartbeats shared, the space we bear.

A Symphony of Solitude

In solitude, melodies emerge,
Notes of longing begin to surge.
A symphony played in quiet delight,
Echoing softly through the night.

In the chamber of dreams, I hear the sound,
Each silent moment, profoundly profound.
With every breath, a song takes flight,
In the stillness, shadows become light.

Solitude wraps its arms around,
Embracing the soft, unspoken ground.
In every pause, a story to tell,
A symphony in silence, woven so well.

Ripples of Enduring Love

In quiet moments, hearts entwine,
Echoes of laughter, gentle and fine.
Through stormy seas, we find our way,
Love's steadfast flame will never sway.

With every glance, a story told,
A tapestry woven with threads of gold.
Through time's embrace, we stand as one,
Two souls united, never undone.

A whisper soft, a touch so dear,
In the silence, I hold you near.
Together we face what life will bring,
In ripples of love, forever we sing.

Seasons will change, but we remain,
In the warmth of trust, there's no more pain.
Our hearts like rivers, winding and free,
Flowing together, just you and me.

As stars bear witness to our shared dance,
Each moment cherished, a fleeting chance.
In every heartbeat, our love resounds,
Enduring echoes, forever found.

In the Embrace of Each Other

In twilight's glow, we find our space,
Lost in the warmth of your sweet grace.
A gentle touch, hands intertwine,
In the embrace, all fears decline.

Whispers of hope in the night's still air,
Wrapped in a silence that's soft and rare.
Every heartbeat, a rhythm pure,
In your arms, I find my cure.

Through life's maze, we wander near,
With a bond that brings us cheer.
In the dance of day and night,
Together, we create our light.

A shelter built from dreams we share,
In each other's eyes, there's nothing to scare.
Through laughter's joy and sorrow's tide,
In the embrace, our worlds collide.

In the tapestry of moments spent,
Every second, a love letter sent.
In the embrace of each other tight,
We craft our story, forever bright.

Our Collective Mosaic

Every piece a story, vibrant and bold,
Together we shine, in colors retold.
Fragments of laughter, sorrow, and grace,
In our mosaic, each finds their place.

Threads of experience woven so tight,
A beautiful quilt stitched with light.
In diverse patterns, we find our song,
In this grand tapestry, we all belong.

From whispers of love to echoes of pain,
In every piece, there's so much to gain.
Cultures and tales, a rich dialogue,
In our collective mosaic, we will not clog.

Through trials faced and joys we share,
The beauty of us is woven with care.
In unity's strength, we rise and we stand,
In this cherished mosaic, hand in hand.

With colors entwined, we shape our fate,
In every heartbeat, we celebrate.
Together we flourish, diverse and bright,
A legacy woven, in love's pure light.

A Dance of Familiar Faces

In crowded rooms, our eyes align,
With familiar warmth, our spirits intertwine.
Each smile a gesture, a story retold,
In this dance of love, we break the mold.

Footsteps echo to a tune so sweet,
We sway through memories that can't be beat.
In laughter's embrace, we spin around,
In the dance of life, joy can be found.

Every glance shared is a gentle caress,
In the twirl of connection, we feel so blessed.
With rhythms that pulse through night's gentle haze,
We lose ourselves in this familiar craze.

Through seasons of change, we hold on tight,
In the dance of familiar faces, all feels right.
With hearts wide open, we take a bow,
In this moment together, we live in the now.

As the music fades, we linger still,
In the warmth of each other, our hearts feel the thrill.
So let's dance together under the moon's embrace,
Forever connected in this sacred space.

Heartstrings Entwined

In quiet moments, we find our way,
Whispers of love in the soft light of day.
Two souls dancing in gentle embrace,
Fate brings us closer, time can't erase.

In the chaos, our hearts intertwine,
Threads of connection, a bond so divine.
Through trials and triumphs, we stand side by side,
Together we blossom, in love we abide.

Every heartbeat echoes a sweet serenade,
A melody woven, never to fade.
Through laughter and tears, we face what we must,
In faith and in hope, together we trust.

Hand in hand, we chase dreams anew,
With passion ignited, we rise like the dew.
Under the stars, our promises glow,
In the tapestry of life, our colors flow.

So here's to the journey, wherever it leads,
In the garden of love, we plant our seeds.
With every heartbeat, our story refines,
Forever, dear love, our heartstrings entwined.

Embracing the Unspoken

In the silence, our souls intertwine,
A language of glances, no need for a sign.
Words left unspoken, yet understood clear,
In the depths of our hearts, you draw near.

A gentle touch sparks a powerful flame,
In this sacred dance, we're both never the same.
In the still of the night, our fears fade away,
In the hush of the moment, we learn how to stay.

Like shadows that flicker beneath the moon's glow,
We navigate paths no one else could know.
Together we wander, uncharted terrain,
In the silence of love, there's no hint of pain.

Through laughter and tears, we bond even tight,
Seeing the beauty in darkness and light.
In the echo of heartbeats, our truth boldly shines,
In the language of souls, we write our designs.

With every unspoken, a promise we weave,
In the fabric of life, in dreams we believe.
Together we stand with a love that's profound,
Embracing the silence, in solace we're found.

A Symphony of Laughter

In moments of joy, our spirits take flight,
A symphony rising in pure delight.
With every chuckle, we dance to the beat,
Creating a rhythm that's honest and sweet.

Through tickles and jokes, we travel as one,
In the warmth of our laughter, shadows are spun.
With no fear of sorrow, we lift each other's gaze,
In the melody of laughter, we find our praise.

With friends gathered 'round, the world feels so light,
A chorus of cheer, making everything bright.
In the echoes of giggles, our hearts sing along,
Finding comfort and joy in the bond of our song.

When storms of life come, we stand side by side,
With laughter as armor, in love we confide.
Through every jest shared, our spirits entwine,
A melody crafted in a love so divine.

As the years roll on, our laughter still grows,
Like petals that open when the soft breeze blows.
In this symphony crafted with love as our guide,
We cherish the laughter, forever our pride.

The Light We Share

In the dawn's embrace, we rise with the sun,
Together we shine, two hearts beating as one.
Through the darkest of nights, your glow is my guide,
In the tapestry woven, love won't divide.

With every shared glance, our spirits ignite,
A flame intertwined, casting shadows of light.
In laughter and joy, our hearts softly glow,
Through trials and triumphs, our love starts to flow.

When the world feels heavy, and burdens are great,
In the warmth of your love, I patiently wait.
You brighten my path with a radiant flare,
In the journey of life, it's the light that we share.

From the stars in the sky to the dew on the leaves,
In both simple moments and grandest of dreams.
Together we wander, hand in hand we dare,
In this beautiful dance, it's the love that we share.

So here's to the sparkle that echoes our truths,
In the depths of our dreams, it's our children's roots.
Forever and always, in moments so rare,
In the light that we shine, it's the love that we share.

Under the Canopy of Love

Beneath the trees' warm embrace,
Whispers of hearts intertwine,
Sunlight dances in soft grace,
In this moment, you are mine.

Leaves above, a gentle quilt,
Nature's breath sings sweet and low,
Every secret, every wilt,
In the shade, true feelings grow.

Time stands still in this space,
With every heartbeat, we belong,
Lost in joy, lost in grace,
Together, we are strong.

Petals fall, the world slows down,
As laughter echoes through the trees,
In this haven, love's our crown,
A whispered promise on the breeze.

Underneath this bough and vine,
We find solace, hand in hand,
A world that's solely yours and mine,
Forever, here we stand.

Fireside Reflections

Crackling embers glow so bright,
Shadows dance upon the walls,
In the warmth of this quiet night,
A gentle peace within us calls.

Moments shared by flickering flame,
Stories whispered, hearts laid bare,
Each soft laugh and every name,
In this glow, we breathe the air.

Cups are filled with dreams and hopes,
Thoughts as rich as the dark roast,
Together we navigate life's slopes,
In this warmth, we cherish most.

Outside, the world may chill and freeze,
But here, the love is ever warm,
With every crackle, we find ease,
Embraced by friendship's tender form.

Let the night stretch long and wide,
As sparks leap to the moonlit sky,
In this moment, let love abide,
Fireside reflections, you and I.

The Bridge Between Us

Two hearts beating, side by side,
A bridge of trust we've built so strong,
Through every storm, through every tide,
Together, we will carry on.

With every step on this shared path,
We weave our dreams as the instances flow,
A love that dances, breaking wrath,
In the light, our spirits grow.

Here lies a bond that time can't sever,
A tapestry, threads intertwined,
In every challenge, we find forever,
In this journey, our souls aligned.

Mountains high and valleys low,
We navigate with hearts aglow,
Through laughter bright and tears like rain,
Together we rise, together we gain.

So let us walk this bridge, my dear,
Hand in hand, we'll face it all,
In the silence, let love steer,
Everready to catch our fall.

Solace in Unity

In every shadow, we find light,
Together, we rise from fall,
With hearts entwined, we face the night,
In our strength, we stand tall.

Voices merge as one sweet song,
With melodies stitched in the air,
In unity, we all belong,
In this love, we find our care.

Through trials faced and fears embraced,
With hands held tight, we forge ahead,
In each challenge, hope is chased,
In every word, love's thread.

Together, we overcome the strife,
Finding solace in every touch,
In this bond, we share our life,
A testament that means so much.

So let us face the world as one,
With open hearts and spirits free,
In unity, we've just begun,
For together, we are meant to be.

Milton Keynes UK
Ingram Content Group UK Ltd.
UKHW021208261024
450281UK00007B/98